MW00949399

Thank you for caring!

Best wishes,

Jane Cory
2014

Published by: Jane S. Foy

Book Design by: Imagine Design, Lorena Perez

Illustrations by: Mónica L. Suárez

Photo by : Mary T. Miller.

First Printing edition 2019

This book is dedicated to all
those caring for a person with any
form of dementia.
You are heroes.
And to Pat.

The A-Z Guide
For
Primary Care Givers
Of
Dementia Patients.

JANE S. FOY

Introduction

This book was written to help you and your loved one, hereafter known as your LO!

I think I have probably been writing it in my head for many years. Long before my LO and I entered the office of a neuropsychologist, I had seen signs of diminished memory and judgment. He underwent a battery of tests in 2013 which gave a name to it: vascular dementia, irreversible and progressive.

Since then, he has had "dips" as I call them. A new lower level of cognition. Sometimes the dip is temporary; other times, it becomes the new normal. (See New Normal under "N")

He also has atrial fibrillation, or AFIB and two years after the dementia diagnosis he had a stroke. Fortunately, there was no paralysis, but he spent time in the Neurology ICU, the Acute Care Hospital and then a rehabilitation facility.

Since the stroke his balance is not quite 100 percent, and he walks slowly. That summer he also had to have two teeth removed. Then, to prevent another stroke, it was determined he should have a Watchman implant, a procedure in which a device is inserted into the left atrial appendage, a sac that doesn't do anything but get you in trouble. With AFIB, the blood does not get pushed through the arteries as it should and can settle or pool in this sack. Then a piece - a clot - breaks off and can travel to the brain, causing another stroke. After my LO's implant, they put him under again, so they could put a camera down his throat to check that the implant was working. In the fall of that year he came down with a doozie of a case of shingles. We were out of town. It was a mess and months later he still had the occasional pain associated with post shingle neuralgia. After that, he had a Squamous carcinoma removed from his calf and a Basal cell carcinoma removed from his forehead, with a little plastic surgery thrown in. He has also had cataract surgery.

Except for some occasional post-shingles pain, he does not remember any of this. I do.

We have been clients of family practitioners, cardiologists, neurologists, ophthalmologists, neuro surgeons, occupational and speech therapists, dental surgeons, dermatologists, plastic surgeons and podiatrists -- all in one year.

He does not make the appointments to see all these people, he cannot drive himself to these appointments, nor can he buy or manage the ensuing pharmaceuticals for the various problems. I do.

He doesn't remember to call his kids, and he has no clue when their birthdays are. He frequently forgets the names of his grand-children and has no idea he has four great-grandchildren.

However, we still take a driving vacation to Florida each spring and make other weekend-driving trips. We go to the movies and concerts, visit with friends and try to have a normal life.

That's my job. Keep in touch with everyone and try to keep it normal. Try to keep the fun and zaniness in our lives.

I am not a doctor or a professional counselor. I am merely the wife of a man who is not the same person I married.

This has been a new experience for both of us, even though I am more aware than he is about how much our lives have changed.

I wrote this book to give a hand to anyone else who is going through this process.

I have no "answers." There is no cure. But, maybe within these pages you'll find some helpful hints to make your situation a little easier.

So, from A to Z, here is a collection of some things I have learned. I hope you can find something you can use in your own life with your LO.

With love and hope,

Jane

Acknowledge: What your LO has is progressive and irreversible. Acceptance may be delayed on your part and on the part of your LO.

Adaptive aids: Post-It notes, labels, and longer handwritten notes with directions will be helpful for a while. At one point you will discover that writing out directions is an exercise that only makes YOU feel better.

We had a rather unusual "appliance" year. Our vacuum, coffee pot and dishwasher all went "kaput" within a few weeks of each other. That meant new operating instructions for the new appliances, and new technology does not come easy, if at all, to a dementia patient. My LO cannot operate the coffee pot or the dishwasher. He won't vacuum unless I am around because he can't remember where the new "on-off" button is.

In two years, he has never learned how to use the new microwave. Instead of hitting the "beverage" button, he hits the clock button, which does nothing for his coffee and requires me to re-set the clock a couple of times a day. Eventually, I expect to have to unplug the microwave when I am gone for fear he tries to heat a cup of coffee for an hour, instead of a minute.

Remind family and friends not to waste money on what they might think of as an adaptive aid that will be "easy" for your LO to operate. People might be tempted to offer voice-controlled phones, or voice recognition speakers, such as Echo, or Alexa. However, unless you're dealing with very early on-set dementia, your LO will not get it.

A very helpful, low-tech aid we received was made by one of my sisters. She cut out card stock slightly larger than a 4 x 6" picture, punched two holes on one side and then glued pictures on each page, and then labeled them. She attached the pictures with two removable rings. The pictures were of family members, places my LO had been, old and new friends and pets! We have added to it several times as the family grows, and we've had new experiences. We keep it on the coffee table and refer to it frequently. If he seems puzzled about news of his granddaughter, I just show him the picture memory book and it all comes back to him.

Advocacy: There are many organizations that advocate for people with dementia. I've listed some of them at the end of the book. But, I have learned that as the primary caregiver, YOU must be the advocate for your loved one. I have learned that although it is important to be polite, it is also very important to be determined. Example: we had an appointment with a dermatologist, but we were kept in the waiting room far too long. When I made the follow-up appointment, I explained to the receptionist that dementia patients do not "wait well." If I make an appointment for 2 p.m., I must be seen at 2 p.m. If the doctor is running late, call me. There is the distinct possibility that if my LO must wait for more than 15 minutes, he will leave the room. Most of the time, if you warn office staff ahead of time, they comply. This inability to wait applies at restaurants as well. My LO loves to go out to a restaurant for lunch. I have learned that diners are a great choice. They serve food…fast! It doesn't feel like a fast food joint because you get a menu. (even though your LO may no longer read menus). My LO peruses the menu and then says something like, "It all looks good, you choose for me." Find a place you know will get your food to you quickly. It used to be that we had a cocktail or glass of wine as we waited for our meal, or wine with dinner. Those days are over. Your LO may be allowed alcohol, mine isn't. And, chances are you'll be driving home, so best to save the adult beverages for home.

As the advocate, be sure to have access to all bank accounts and credit card accounts; you will also have to keep your LO's credit cards in your possession. Make sure you have access to utility company accounts and insurance (including Social Security). Anything that has your LO's name on it, should also have your name on it.

This process is tedious and time consuming. I remember being so frustrated when I had to put my LO on the phone to verify that I was to be included on his account for any inquiries or transactions. I had to stand there with the phone on "speaker" and prompt him through the call.

Appearance: (yours) My LO has dementia, that's why I look like a hag. No, no and NO! There are any number of "yeah, but…" excuses. You don't let yourself go to the dogs because your LO has dementia. You let yourself go to the hairdresser, the manicurist, the masseuse or esthetician. My LO has dementia so I schedule a monthly facial, a monthly massage and a weekly manicure. Plus, I get my hair re-blonded every 5 weeks. I am not selfish. I am not self-centered. I am a caregiver and I am going to make certain I look the best I can for me, and for him. So, take the time, each day, to do your hair and if you wear it, put on a little make-up (probably just women on the make-up thing, but whatever). Your LO will probably start to get forgetful about is his or her own personal hygiene and choice of clothing. That will become another one of your jobs: making sure your LO is clean and doesn't have pajama bottoms on instead of pants. You set an example. Your LO will notice and you can use your own spiffy appearance to convince your LO that it's bath time! You will also feel much better.

Bills: We will mention $$$ in various forms throughout this book. If you think you are going to run into financial difficulty (paying monthly utility bills, credit card payments, mortgage, etc.) GET HELP NOW! That may mean a pow-wow with family members, a chat with your bank and credit card companies, or a conference with a social worker.

Boredom: I have found that my LO is not capable of entertaining himself, beyond of reading his newspapers, walking the dog and performing a couple of other daily rituals. The imagination or creativity is just not there. Add to your list of titles: Social Director. One day I noticed him moping around the house, so I invited him to go to a department store with me. He grudgingly said he might as well as there was nothing else to do. I suggested to go across the street to our community garden plot and do a little weeding. His reply: "That's not in my program." Really? That line has been shared with many friends and family. We have all decided that when we are asked to do something

15

we don't want to do, we simply say, "That's not in my program."
Ya gotta laugh.

One way to alleviate boredom is to have someone come and visit. My
LO is very reluctant to have a stranger stop by. He is shy about having
someone he doesn't know around him and he doesn't want to pay
anyone! On the other hand, friends and family are usually welcome. If
someone he knows offers to pop in for an hour on a weekly basis, I'll go
for it. At some point, I'll make the decision on my own to get part-time
help in the form of a paid companion.

Breathing: This is a simple way to reduce or control stress. There is
much to be said for deep breathing, whether it's a Yoga class, or simply
sitting quietly by yourself before you go to sleep. Breathe deeply for a
couple of minutes. There are many books out there to help you develop a
breathing routine. Sounds funny, doesn't it? We breathe naturally, right?
Well, I have found that one of the ways I know I'm stressed is when I hold
my breath. Test yourself; you may find that you hold your breathe more
than you think you do. So, in those moments of tension, stop and take in
three big breaths!

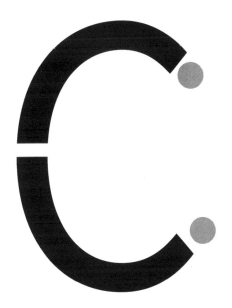

Counseling: You need to be as mentally healthy as you can be. If your guilt, resentment, anger, or frustration is getting the better of you, it's time to chat with a professional. Maybe it's a psychologist or psychiatrist; your Doctor will be able to recommend someone. The Alzheimer's Association has support sessions to help you deal with your care giving challenges. And some elder- care companies, such as Home Instead, have classes for the caregiver. There are, also, your friends and family members, and clergy. But sometimes, an objective outsider who knows the care giving business is often a good choice. Talking to yourself rarely gets any results. I've tried it!

Cuddle: Regardless of whatever else your physical relationships includes; hugs and cuddles are important to you and your LO. And a kiss hello and good-bye, and a few in between are good for you both!

Notes and Reminders

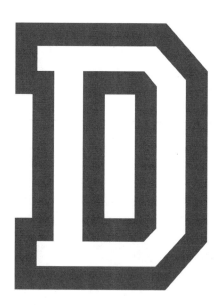

Death: What do you want to happen to your body after you die? If you can't answer that for yourself, how will you answer it for your LO? My LO has always had a very pragmatic attitude toward death. Many years before he was diagnosed with dementia, he found an article in an AARP magazine. He cut it out and wrote in the margin: "Jane, I want this." Below that he signed his name. It was an article about donating your remains to medical research. It gave instructions on how to contact agencies in your state that collect the bodies of the deceased and send them off to a medical school for research. If you arrange this in advance, it all occurs very quickly after death. Afterward, maybe up to a year later, the cremated remains are sent to the survivor. We signed up. Then we let our families know what we did. It's also written in our will.

That might not be your idea of a send-off. But, your LO will not be able to tell you what his/her desires are if they are in the late stages of dementia. Get it arranged now.

This is especially important when it comes to dealing with your LO's family. Be sure they know what your LO wants, because the last thing you'll need is a discussion about what a family member "thinks" your LO would have wanted. It's a good idea to send emails to family members each time a milestone decision is made. Print the email and save it.

Doctors: A good relationship with your primary care doctor is key. Chances are your LO, like mine, has additional issues outside of the dementia. You will accompany your LO to the Doc's office and will be the translator. The Doc asks, "How are you?" The dementia patient says, "Just fine." You'll be there to tell the Doc the truth.

If your LO has other health issues, you probably have seen a specialist or two, or you might have to see one in the future. Your Primary Care Doc is your point person. Be sure he/she is in the loop with any other Doc you have, and that includes dentists, optometrists and chiropractors, and any other health professional. DO NOT assume that any of them, even with the best of intentions, will communicate with your Primary Care Doc. This is especially important if your LO is hospitalized. When my LO had a stroke, I gave the hospital our Primary Care Doc's info, but, my LO was in rehab before I realized his Primary Care doc knew nothing about it. It turned out that the info on my LO's stroke and subsequent treatment was not shared because his primary care doctor was affiliated with another hospital.

I was furious.

As for specialists: We had semi-annual appointments with a neurologist and a cardiologist. Our neurologist would give him a verbal memory test, which he would fail. He did not remember her from one appointment to the next. She prescribed the only medication (at the time) on the market for dementia. That was the only care she provided until I asked her why we needed to see her at all. She said my LO should have a neurologist of record to call in the event there was another "episode." I replied that if there is another "episode," I would call 911, and the neurologist of record would be the one we'd meet in the emergency room. Our Primary Care doc now prescribes the dementia meds. Same thing with the cardiologist. On our twice-a-year visits her physician assistant took my LO's vitals, and then the cardiologist came into the exam room and listened to his heart, only to proclaim that he was in AFIB. Yep, we knew that. He has meds for that, and our primary care doc can prescribe them.

Treating skin cancer was something only the dermatologist could do, so we kept our follow-up appointments with her. The point here is this that if your LO must see a specialist, so be it. But, if the visits are not productive, let the Primary Care Doc take over. If the time comes when your LO must see or re-visit a specialist, your Primary Care Doc will let you know. Meantime, the fewer appointments, waiting rooms and questionnaires you and your LO must deal with, the better. Remember, you are now in charge of all the insurance paper work as well.

Making and getting to appointments may take you away from your job, if you work outside the home. Trying to juggle that schedule is stressful, so make sure the medical care you receive is the medical care you need.

Recently, my LO told me he no longer likes his doctor. He is not able to tell me why, but I think it is because his doctor has not made him "better." Dementia patients can develop a "grudge" against people they have known for years. And what is maddening is that a guy he NEVER cared for is suddenly, "a nice fellow!" Don't expect things to make sense all or part of the time.

Remember: Dementia is a disease, not an attitude.

Find out from your Doctor if there is a Memory Clinic in your area. Many medical schools offer them.

Be sure your Doctor is aware that you are the caregiver. He/she should be monitoring your health as well.

Documents: Get everything in order. Wills, power of attorney, etc. Find the deed to your home if you have one, all insurance policies, and any other legal documents you have. Review them, making sure everything is current and correct. And look them over every few months. Things change. Be prepared. (See Family). Be sure you have a designated executor to take over if you should suddenly be incapacitated.

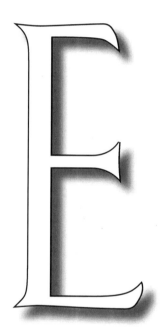

Embarrassment: With close friends and family your LO might even joke about memory loss. But, in front of strangers, you will notice he/she will avoid conversation so as not to reveal their confusion or their inability to find the right word. They might even be short with people who ask direct questions. Lively dinners conversations with guests might be cut short by your LO if he/she can't keep up. My LO sometimes claims he is tired and excuses himself to go to bed. Embarrassment might be the reason there is resistance to meeting new people.

Your LO will also realize there are things he can't do and will be embarrassed by that. One weekend we attended a wedding. He tied his necktie perfectly. I was surprised. But the next weekend we attended another function and he could not complete the knot. I was no help. I just told him that his tie looked fine the way it was, and he really didn't need one anyway. At the function he removed the tie. I should probably learn to tie at least one type of knot. Sigh.

Emotions: Try to keep them on an even keel. A calm voice and a calm demeanor will have a calming effect on your loved one. If you are behaving erratically, your loved one will pick up on it. (see Venting). Your LO may ask you the same question many, many times over, sometimes within the space of a minute! You answer the question the 10th time, just as you did the first time. If your LO could remember he asked the question before, he wouldn't be asking again. Your LO has a memory problem. He is NOT trying to annoy you!

Remember to tell relatives and friends to do the same thing. Tell them how to deal with the repetitive questions. If you notice someone is not capable of being patient with your LO, that person should be avoided. If they don't get it, move on to people who do.

Exercise: Going to work, the grocery store, doing the laundry, running up and down the stairs to change the TV channel because your LO doesn't remember how to do it. None of it counts as exercise. That's not fair, but life is not fair. You need to get exercise.

Lots of caregiving advice has to do with what you are doing for yourself. I LOVE my girlfriends, and I love to have the occasional cocktail with them. And yes, that's something I do for myself. But, the best thing you can do for yourself is get off to a gym, Yoga class, or a 30-minute daily walk.

I found I was in a rut with my daily care giving routine and gained 25 pounds. Not good. I needed to get out on my own to work on my physical well-being. It wasn't easy, and I knew I would get pushback from my LO. He had been a personal trainer, so we have equipment in the our "workout" room, but I have always hated it. It was designed for him and his clients. And I knew if I told him I needed to work out he would want me to use his equipment AND be at home with him.

However, some years ago, I had taken a weekly Yoga class, which I very much enjoyed. So, instead of telling my LO I had joined a gym, I told him I was taking a yoga class. That's something he can't teach and doesn't understand, but knows I liked it. So, he was very encouraging, rather than being stubborn about my working out at home. There is an element of "truthiness" (thank you, Stephen Colbert)in my explanation because the gym I joined has a yoga studio in the back. I haven't used it yet. I might though. Someday.

Your LO needs exercise as well. Walking the dog if you have one or taking walks with you. You can develop floor exercises that are within range of his/her ability, or you can develop chair exercises. If you have respite care, be sure to right out the exercise plan, so that person can participate in the routine.

Extemporaneousness: I made up that word. It means that if it is AT ALL possible when your LO says, "Do you want to go somewhere?", you say, "You bet!" One afternoon as I was writing this my LO came to me and said we should go out and do something. I left the writing, the laundry, the weeding, and the making of soup, did a fast make-up job, threw on a cute hat, got doggie treats and water for the pup, and we were out the door! All in all, a very good idea. And I assured him it was HIS idea. Being spontaneous is a treat, and unfortunately it won't last long. Enjoy it and go do something!

Family: Well. How many books have been written about family dynamics? This is not one more. Here's what I can advise: At the beginning, when your LO is diagnosed, gather as many family members as you can in one place. (That was not possible for us, so I did a group email. I sent it to my family and his.) Explain what the diagnosis is and don't leave out any facts, such as: "This is progressive and irreversible." Hard stuff to hear but it needs to be shared. Explain the meds your LO is taking, and restrictions on your LO such as, no driving, horseback riding, climbing ladders, etc. Tell these folks what you need NOW. Next, provide web addresses for organizations such as the Alzheimer's Association or any other trusted resource that specializes in your LO's kind of dementia issue. This is important because it is not your responsibility to educate others about your LO's condition. You are educating yourself about one case, your LO's.

If you hear comments such as, "He seems to be getting better," you'll know the speaker hasn't read the material. You are not required to give the whole family daily, weekly or monthly updates. I have found that an update after a periodic medical check-up or when the LO's condition changes is enough. Otherwise, siblings, offspring, etc., will need to check in with you. It is VERY important, however, to contact the family if YOUR needs change.

Fear: My LO has not expressed fear of anything, although I know he is fearful of my being absent. However, I have heard from friends who have dealt with elderly relatives, especially women, who become fearful of all sorts of things. One dear lady became fearful of the shower/bathtub. That can lead to all sorts of problems. The fears are real and have to be dealt with, whether through direct guidance or active avoidance. Your doctor may be able to help.

Filters: Behavioral filters start disappearing and sometimes it's not polite or nice. I joined a service organization that has a dining room, bar and swimming pool. Lots of older people belong. I thought it might be fun for him to be around people his own age. We had an unfortunate experience with rotten service the first time we went there for dinner. LO had been in the restaurant business before he became a personal trainer, and he was so annoyed he said he would never go back because "those people are old and fat." I had to get a bit firm with him and told him he might not be fat, but he was old! I added that I would not tolerate his being rude to fat or old people and that in the future I would enjoy the place by myself or with my friends. He has since reluctantly gone to the pool with me. Once he gets there he enjoys himself. Don't look for rational thought.

Finances: These will probably come under your complete control. Simply put: Find out who owes what and to whom. If you and your LO have separate bank accounts, either combine them or get yourself on your LO's account. You will be paying all the bills, so make sure you know when they are due and from which account they are paid. In addition to everything else going on, you don't want to hurt your credit rating by missing payments. (see Bills)

Food: If you work or must be away from home during a mealtime, you have to start thinking about easy food that does not require cooking. I always have cereal, milk and bananas or other fruit available. Individual cartons of coconut water (great way to combat de-hydration), yogurt, hummus or string cheese are easy and relatively nutritious. Low-salt whole grain or rice crackers are also good snacks. Using one slice of whole grain bread, you can make little sandwiches with nut butters, cottage cheese, cream cheese, etc. These are good things to have in the pantry or refrigerator, especially if you are absent for a few hours.

Friends: If your friends were your LO's friends before the Illness, they will remain your friends, but might find it difficult relating to your LO's memory loss. Some people are not equipped to be around someone with mental issues. Your social life will change.

Be sure to prepare your friends, especially ones you have not seen for a while, what your LO's current condition is.

Notes and Reminders

Gifts: (See technology). What to get the LO for Christmas and birthday, Mother's or Father's Day, etc. Everyone is different, but one constant: people like to eat. If people ask what to get your LO, tell them a gift card to a favorite restaurant would be great. Or, a gift card to a grocery store to get the LO something that is a favorite. My LO loves chocolate milk! Cash is very helpful for a variety of necessities. Gift cards to theaters are very welcomed. Books are iffy because reading will become difficult. But, big photo books of places your LO has been are great.

A word about gift cards. We encountered great confusion when my LO was given a VISA gift card. I explained to him that it was worth $50. He immediately wanted to go to the bank to get the cash. I spent a lot of time explaining to him that he could BUY something for $50, but he could not "cash it in" for $50. This became a kind of circular conversation until he became exasperated, handed the thing to me and said, "Get yourself something," and walked away. Perhaps more specific gift cards would be a better idea.

Now, what about you?

During a crisis-situation, as when my LO was hospitalized for his stroke, I got lots of, "What can I do?"

I do not mean to sound like an ingrate, but let's think about this for a moment. My husband is in the Neuro ICU. I have more on my mind than I can deal with, not including who is going to take the dog out, and oh by the way Mister My Boss at work, I won't be seeing you for a while. And you ask what can you do? So now I need to solve your problem, too? Jeez. Use your imagination!! Buy groceries, walk the dog, hire a cleaning service, rake the leaves. The list goes on.

I got some very good advice from a sister. Just reply, "What did you have in mind.?"

When the uncle of a friend of mine died, and she had to travel a distance for the service, I asked her when she would be back. She told me, and I said, "Well dinner will be taken care of for that evening. I'll call you before I deliver." This was the same woman who brought me a basket of shower and bath soaps and creams and other wonderful stuff when I was spending 12 hours a day the hospital.

The people who have always remembered you on your birthday or other special days will continue to remember you.

Others won't. So be it.

Health: Yours. This may be the most important part of this book. People have said to me, "Oh, you must be exhausted." NO, I AM NOT!! Why? Because I get eight hours of sleep a night with a nap thrown in for good measure. I am not Einstein but even I can figure out that if you are using up more energy caring for a loved one, you better be manufacturing more energy by giving your body and mind the rest they need. Make sure you get your annual physical. Women, get your gynie check-up and your mammogram. See your dentist and your eye doctor. (Refer to Counseling and see Exercise)

Hotels: I have learned that it is best for my LO and me if we stay In a hotel when we are traveling, rather than staying with family. Unless your hosts have a suite with a private bath, it's easier to avoid accidents if you have a hotel room. We once stayed at a relative's home in a guest room, but the bathroom was out the door and down the hall. Fortunately, I woke up from a sound sleep just before he was about to use the walk-in closet as a bathroom. Imagine everyone's embarrassment.

Most hotel rooms come with a small refrigerator which is also helpful for bedtime snacks, and early- morning bowls of cereal. And, of course, the hotel room TV, where your LO can watch his or her choice of programs, is key.

Housework: Not nearly as important as your health, but clutter and disarray will cause confusion for your LO. If you can afford the occasional cleaning service, it is well worth the price. (Hint: A great gift idea!) If not, get yourself any one of those de-cluttering books or spring- cleaning books that have flooded the market. As a matter of fact, an activity I have found my LO likes is when we go through boxes of old stuff, papers, mementos, pictures, etc. Unless your LO is an incurable hoarder, he will enjoy keeping the good stuff and pitching the stuff that is not important.

If there are simple household chores your LO can do such as dusting, vacuuming, loading and unloading the dishwasher, it's a win-win. We purchased a very lightweight vacuum so my LO could vacuum the three floors of our townhouse. It's not the best vacuum, and of course, he doesn't know how to empty the full cannister, but he feels he is contributing. It doesn't matter if the vacuuming or dusting is perfect.

Hygiene: Your LO will begin to forget to use shampoo in the shower and eventually will forget to use body soap as well. The only way to be completely sure he is using soap is to be there with him. That may not always be possible. However, a person can get fairly clean with warm water. You'll have to monitor teeth cleaning and use of deodorant as well. How you do this is up to you, but remember that this is something to add to your ever- growing list.

I means you: I am responsible for my LO, I oversee my loved one's well-being, I am in control of our lives. I will reach out for help to accomplish the above. I will tell people I am a caregiver.

Idiosyncrasies: (see Filters). There are some topics or issues that become a constant topic of conversation. My LO has little tolerance for obese people. He doesn't really give a hoot why they are overweight; he just doesn't approve. He mentions this to me wherever there are numerous people who are large, including restaurants or grocery stores. So far, he comments quietly. He cannot stand animated TV or movies. I took him to see "The Secret Lives of Pets" and we had to leave early. He thought I had played a joke on him. The only way I could get him to stop complaining was to get him a gelato. That or regular ice cream will usually calm things. Generally, the last TV show he watches before bedtime is the News Hour on PBS. So, when the TV goes on the next day around 4 p.m., the same PBS station comes on, but it's airing an animated children's educational show. He will come and get me and ask me to "get rid of those kids." He loves kids! He hates animation. Our doctor says that quirk is the first time he's heard of "anti-animation!"

In general, when your LO develops unique tendencies, you'll have to be mindful of them, especially in social situations.

Notes and Reminders

Journal: Journaling is more than just jotting down your thoughts, although that's a very therapeutic activity. In addition, it's a good idea to jot down what you observe about your LO, and the changes that are occurring. This is valuable information to share with your LO's doctor and family members.

Juggling: Yes, you will have many balls in the air. From my experience, it helps to keep your lives as uncomplicated as possible. That's different for everyone but keeping it simple really helps. That means, by the way, learning to say, no!

JANE FOY

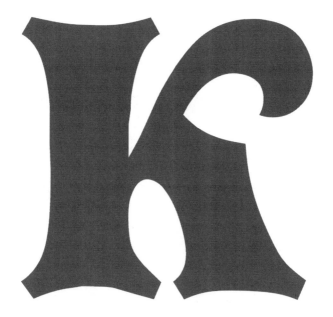

44

Kindness: My LO is incredibly sensitive to the kindness of others. A firm handshake, a friendly comment, or a little assistance goes a long way toward putting a dementia patient at ease. The opposite is true as well, unfortunately. As much as the memory is fading, any perceived slight is not forgotten. Sometimes this can become a fixation. At that point, you must deal with the situation lovingly, but firmly.

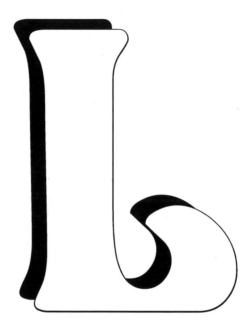

Laugh: If you don't have a good laugh with your LO once a day, at least, figure out a way to make that happen. Better than pills.

Lies: Outright lying to your LO, as with anyone, will eventually get you in trouble. Your LO will surprise you with his occasional recollections and/or rational thought. So be careful; even if you are not sharing the facts 100%, always include that element of "truthiness" in what you say.

Refer to "Exercise" for my best example!

Limitations: Your LO has limitations brought on by the illness. You must put limitations on yourself to keep your mind clear and your body healthy. I am not talking about denying yourself something. I am talking about limiting yourself. Let's look at your "to-do" list. How many items are on it? Do they all have to be done today? How about spreading them out over the week? And how about not going nuts if one item doesn't get accomplished? And if there is something that you absolutely need, order it on line, have it delivered, reach out to a friend, or just fuhgeddaboudit.

Loved One: Never lose track of the fact that no matter how challenging your life has become it is your loved one who has the condition. Dementia patients know they are different, and they know you know it.

Notes and Reminders

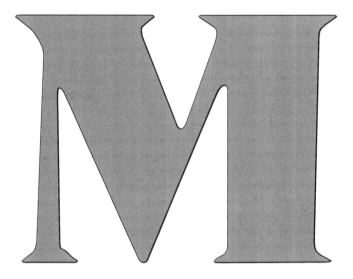

Memory: Well, isn't that what we are talking about? No, not your LO's, yours. You are multitasking. You are constantly planning for the next meal, dispensing of meds, activities…the list goes on. So, of course, you may forget stuff: You forget your cell phone at home or at work. You forget you were supposed to meet friends after work. You forget to send birthday cards or presents.

My LO has never been able to pack a suitcase that included everything he'd need for a week. Once I was so obsessed with making sure he had his suitcase filled with the requisite flip-flops, tennis shoes and underwear that I left all three of my bathing suits on the dresser.

So, I make lists. I try to make a list of meals for 4-5 days ahead. That way my grocery list is not overwhelming. I have reminders about checking on our bank accounts. Automatic payments can be wonderful, but you need to be sure the bills are being paid from the appropriate account. I learned the hard way that my LO had been paying bills out of his savings account,

not his checking account, so when I paid out of the checking account, whoops! Came up short!

I make a list of what repairs need to be done at the house, so I can budget for them. And I list of chores that need to be done on a weekly basis.

If you think of something, write it down in your little notebook. If you get the stuff on the list done, great. If not, don't freak! You will learn to say, "So what!"

New Normal: I first heard this expression from my friend with the Alzheimer's Association. She referred to how your normal daily routine will change, because what your LO can remember and what he or she can do will change from week to week and, eventually, from day to day. Once a task is forgotten, there is no getting it back. Do not be surprised when one day he can no longer remember to take out the trash or do other routine task. Your routines will change repeatedly. When my friend began talking about holiday traditions, the new normal really sunk in. Holidays are not a daily routine, so the changes in your LO will seem exaggerated at holiday times. Changes in your LO's personality and his or her ability to do certain tasks will become very evident during the holidays. Your new normal might include passing up the live Christmas tree search or hiring someone to hang lights on the outside of the house, or even traveling to someone's house for holiday dinner.

We will travel six hours to spend Christmas with my LO's children. He will not remember his grandchildren's names, nor realize who these little ones are crawling around the floor. That would be great-grandchildren.

 He will not remember extended family members, in-laws or new girlfriends or boyfriends. He will have a delightful time, enjoy dinner and expect to go home early. He will be surprised we are spending a couple of nights in a hotel and he will fret over the well-being of the dog. Not exactly normal, but new. All I can recommend is to be flexible and keep it as simple as possible!

New Things: Don't expect new things to go over really well. A new way to prepare chicken: yes. Dining together is one of my LO's favorite activities and he enjoys changes in the menu.

I have found that new clothes are appreciated when my LO receives them, but then he promptly puts them in the back of the closet. I bought him a winter car-coat, so he would have something warm to cover his rear end. He loved it and the matching scarf, but every morning (when I was at work) he would wear his waist-length coat to walk the dog, then tell me how cold he had been during the walk. I would show him the car coat and he would be so delighted to have it. Next morning, same old waist-length coat...

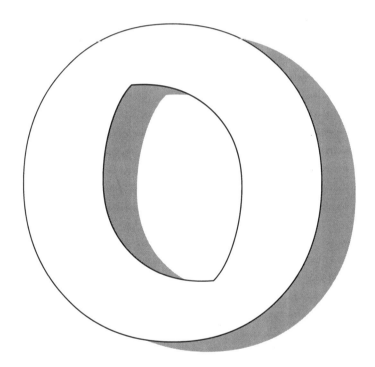

Obsessive: My LO has not become overly obsessive, but he does fixate on things. If we are traveling he will fixate on day/time. No matter how many entries on the calendar or Post-It notes I leave, he will not stop asking me when we are going until we are on the road. In that case I try not to divulge too much information too soon.

Trying to explain relationships is becoming more difficult, but he is fixated on who's who. Me: Harold is your brother Henry's eldest son. LO: My brother is dead. Me: "I know, but his son Harold is not. We're going to a picnic with him today." LO: "But my brother won't be there." You get the picture: Familial relationships are tough for my LO to comprehend; family trees are too much for him. Just explain what your LO really needs to know. One time we went to a picnic and my LO had a long and lively conversation with one of his sisters. When we got back to our hotel he was distraught because he had no idea who she was, and he was sure she was hurt by that. That took a half-hour of conversation to calm him down. And it was a topic of conversation, repeatedly, on the 6-hour drive home. When we returned home I suggested "we" write her a note telling her how delightful it had been to spend time with her. I wrote it, he signed it, and I haven't heard a peep since.

In order to get your LO off a subject he/she might not let go of, find ways to divert the conversation with a distraction. If your LO won't let go of an idea, you can say, "Oh look, there are two blue birds in the yard. Let's go see them." Whatever it is that is completely NOT the fixated topic! Many times if you divert or distract, your LO will not return to the topic.

Opinions: My LO has very strong opinions about certain people, especially politicians. There is a football coach who is on his "bad" list, but not because of his consistent losing seasons. No, my LO never liked him from his first press conference. There are people he has decided he does not care for, but fortunately, at least for now, when he is in their presence, he is polite. I say this with a sort of giggle:

Beware of family reunions. You never know when the filter may develop a hole!

Out and about: An elderly friend of my mother's once told her that she went out for lunch, for bridge or for shopping almost every afternoon while her invalid husband was napping, reading or otherwise content. Some criticized of her for leaving him (although he was quite safe). She explained that if BOTH of them were stuck in the house all day, she would have nothing funny or new to share with him, and she would have nothing to get "gussied up" for. My mother did the same thing when my father became bedridden. A short lunch with friends, a trip to the hairdresser, a shopping excursion. She was able to get out and about and Daddy was happy to see her and hear her stories when she returned. Side note: My dad was not always napping when my Mother was gone. He became addicted to soap operas. Woe unto the wayward child who tried to enter his room while he was watching HIS "stories."

Notes and Reminders

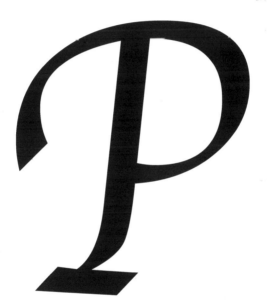

The patient: There can only be one. It's your LO, not you. That is why I stress keeping your spirits up with various beauty treatments, getting lots of sleep, some exercise (some by yourself, some with your LO), a healthy diet, and a fairly regular schedule. You've heard this a million times: If you smoke, quit. It's bad for you and can be worse for your LO. I am all for a restorative cocktail, but drowning your sorrow over caring for a dementia patient in alcohol doesn't help. Easy does it.

Patience: You never know how patient a person you are until you are tested. I think I am sometimes more impatient with myself than I am with my LO. You can cuss at yourself for making some mistake, but you MUST be patient when you're asked to change the TV channel three times while trying to prepare dinner. Take a deep breath, use a calm voice and remember that yesterday he knew how to use the remote. Today he does not.

Personality change: Sometimes good, sometimes not. My LO was in the restaurant business for most of his adult life. Before he was diagnosed he could be a real pain in the neck at a restaurant regarding service. I had to remind him several times over many years that he did not have the right to make other people at the table uncomfortable with his whining about service. These days, he still whines, but not as much and usually a "look" from me will end it. On the other hand, he has developed this thing about clouds. He studies them and is very happy to sit and watch them for quite some time. He never had an interest in that kind of beauty before. He also loves looking at the antics of little kids. He loves it when a youngster is sitting next to us in a restaurant and says hi to him. Perhaps there is just a mellowing that comes with age, and dementia.

Pets: The upside is the pleasure they bring. Caring for an animal (walking, feeding, grooming) can give a person with dementia a purpose.

We know that a relationship with a pet can reduce blood pressure and stress. That is why we see so many pictures of service dogs being taken to assisted living and nursing homes. The downside: they need to be fed regularly, dogs need to be walked, cats need to have their litter box changed. Grooming, veterinarian care and boarding are expensive.

Bottom line: If you can afford a pet, welcome one into your home. There are many shelter animals waiting for a forever home. Keep in mind, you or another family member will have more responsibility toward the pet's upkeep than the dementia patient.

Quiet time: I need it, he doesn't. I had been a radio broadcaster for many years. When I got into my car after work to return home or do errands, I was completely happy with silence. I am not a big TV watcher either. But, he is. If quiet time is important to you, manage a place (in your home or elsewhere) where you get an hour or so of silence.

Sometimes my quiet time is during his nap-time, or while he is watching TV. I can slip downstairs to our family room and close the door. Quiet time is for writing in your journal (which is a good idea!) reading for pleasure or making lists. Maybe even for meditation and deep breathing. Whatever. I think it helps.

Repetitiveness: Same question over and over in a very short span of time. "What time are they coming over?" Same observation over and over. "There sure are a lot of new cars on the road these days." My LO doesn't get the beard fad, especially the ones that are totally unkempt. Not a bearded wonder goes by that he doesn't comment. Then he'll say, "Do you like that look?" I'll say, "I don't care for them on most men and I really don't care for them on women." There will be a beat, and then we both laugh. (see Patience)

Safety: What might your LO do that could possibly injure himself, or someone else? Can your LO shower alone, including adjusting the water temperature? Can he remember to turn the water off? How about shaving? After my LO had his stroke I was advised to get him a battery-operated shaver.

What about the kitchen? My LO never cooked, so I do not have to worry about a stove or oven being left on. But, as mentioned before, he does not operate the microwave correctly. What if he put a cup of coffee in there and instead of hitting 1 minute, he hit 1 hour? That could cause a fire.

If he doesn't understand appliances such as the coffeepot or the microwave, you might want to consider unplugging these devices in your absence.

We no longer use our fireplace. He doesn't remember the procedure for starting and maintaining a fireplace blaze. Although that is pleasant, it is not something I want to add to my list of "to-do's." In warm weather I put a plant on the hearth; in winter I use battery operated candles. The cost of converting to a gas fireplace is costly, but it could be done.

Could your LO lock him or herself out of the house? Do neighbors have keys? Is there a hidden key you can easily get to, or tell someone about?

Driving is out of the question for my LO. Taking a driver's license from a person is tough. He has not mentioned it in quite a while, but there was a time when he was adamant about driving. His doctor and I talked about this and came up with a plan. I told my LO that because of his stroke and his age he would have to retake his driver's test to drive again. I knew he would not go for that. But, he still keeps his license with him and he is still insured. He hasn't mentioned driving for a while.

Be very careful about the location and accessibility of any drugs. That means prescription, over-the-counter and supplements.

You might want to consider a monitor for your LO, and/or for you. We know that some dementia patients will walk out of their home and take off. This has resulted in some tragic incidences. So a monitor for your LO might be a real life-saving apparatus. But, have you thought about what would happen if YOU had an accident or a sudden heart attack? A physician friend of mine told me if you are incapacitated, game over.

Schedules: Understanding of the year, month, day, and time will diminish. Post-It notes and calendars with large spaces to fill in will become part of your décor (We have three of those). When you write things on the calendar your LO may tell you he can't read your writing. That is a ploy to get you to explain the entries on the calendar. Or your LO will just forget to look at the calendar. I came home from work one day to find my LO all gussied up and ready to go out to lunch. He was one week ahead of schedule. He was embarrassed. I told him his eye must have slipped down a row on the calendar, and that he looked very handsome anyway. Befuddled but happy, he changed clothes and came back for lunch at home.

As excited as I get planning and looking forward to vacations and other events, I find it's best to limit discussions about things in the future until almost the last minute. Otherwise things will get confusing, and your LO will ask you a hundred times, "When we are leaving?"

Explain the day's activities one or two elements at a time. For instance, if you have several errands to do, start with one of them. "We have some errands to do today, but first, we need to get your haircut." After that, add another stop on your errand list. Take it step-by-step.

Seasonal Change Over: This is kind of an in joke. I love to change my home décor with the seasons. If I had my way (and the space) I would have four sets of china & glassware, one for each season. Instead, I make slight changes to the house for each season, including: seasonal refrigerator magnets, window vases or candles, centerpiece for dining room table, cloth napkins and placemats or tablecloth, etc. These are little reminders of what month it is and my LO enjoys helping with the changes. It's a little thing, but it's a little pick-me-up for you and your LO. It's also a reality reminder for your LO.

Sense of humor: You need to hang onto yours! And a sense of the absurd is helpful!

Every now and then my LO comes up with something that is funny. Example: I told him a young friend of ours was dismayed that he didn't seem to be able to find a girlfriend.

"Easiest thing in the world," my LO said. "You go around a corner, you find a girl, take her to dinner. Done. Couldn't be simpler."

Our young friend told my LO he must be going around the wrong corner!

This one is funny AND exasperating. There are times when I take a lot of time answering a question, and after I get through the explanation (which I think is pretty clear), he'll say, "Well, I don't know about that," in a manner that sounds like I made the whole thing up!

Sleep: Yes, it's very important for you and your LO, BUT - if your LO is sleeping more than usual (taking 2 naps a day or going to bed at 6:15 p.m.) you should pay attention. This could be the onset of depression or a physical problem. Also, while a sleeping, a person is not getting fluids.

We determined that my LO was dehydrated because he was sleeping so much. I have provided him with a small bottle of water or coconut water for overnight drinks. Check with your doctor to see if you are dealing with a medical/psychological issue.

So what: This is the first cousin to sense of humor. Certain things that seemed important a while ago won't seem so important after a while. If he or she is able to do some household chores, maybe the work won't be done exactly as you would do it - so what? You get the idea.

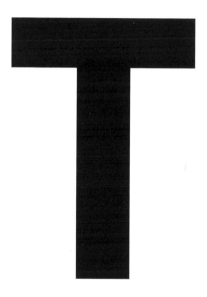

Technology: Don't do it. You cannot teach a dementia person anything new and much of what they used to know will fade away. Do not give them a new phone or new apps for their phone. Do not give them any gadget that requires an owner's manual. One day your LO will make a pot of coffee, the next day the coffee pot will look like a rocket ship to him. One day your LO will call you at work every half hour. The next day, she won't know how to get to her contacts page. Same with the TV. Your LO will eventually forget how to operate the remote. You can write down directions for how to reheat coffee in the microwave or write down which TV stations he likes or show him how all his telephone contacts are on one page, but eventually all this will disappear. So, stand by to help each time. That's just the way it is. Be sure he is safe.

Understanding: In the big picture, you must have an understanding attitude toward your LO for what are going to be many changes and mistakes. That's the big picture. Smaller picture: Don't think you will understand everything your LO says, especially when and if aphasia sets in. My LO and I spend lot of time guessing what he means. It's like a word game. We use all sorts of association tricks to get to what he means, whether it's a word, a person, or a memory. I have found that treating this as calmly as possible reduces his frustration. We will try to find "clues" to what he means. For instance, we loaned friends of ours some books on Ireland, including my journal from our trip there. There was no mention of when they would return the books, but I knew they would. My LO got a little anxious about their return but could not tell me what he was talking about. Finally, he asked me to come to the living room. He pointed to a stack of Ireland books. I then realized he wanted to know where the others were and when they would be returned. This will probably develop into a fixation, so I will have to tell our friends to get the books over here shortly!

Underestimate: Don't underestimate your LO's understanding of his/her condition. My LO has no memory of his stroke, but he knows his mind is not what it once was. Do not underestimate what your LO remembers. I have found on a few occasions that my LO thinks he was slighted by someone because of a casual word, or action. I have no idea where these slights came from and can only assure him that the person he has developed a distrust of is our friend, or really is fond of him. On a couple of occasions such as these I told him had he hurt my feelings by saying he didn't care for a relative or friend. Several hours later, he approached me with an apology. Forgive and move on.

Violence: I am not talking about moderately aggressive behavior or agitation. (Sometimes these are medical conditions which should be shared with your doctor immediately. Urinary tract infections can cause a LO to act out or even just retreat). I am talking about flat-out physical violence. I was told by an Alzheimer's authority that violence is one indicator that a person should be removed from the home. This is SO difficult on several levels. Ceding your role as caregiver can be agonizing, guilt-inducing, and fraught with anxiety. There aren't enough facilities in this country to house people with dementia or Alzheimer's, and besides, such facilities cost oodles of $$$$. Most of us can't afford this care, and as a result, many risk their own safety. If your LO is 50-100 pounds heavier than you are and punches you in the jaw, you will be injured. Even petite women with dementia can bite, scratch and slap. These are some unfortunate realities of your future that could occur and they should be considered a possibility. Remember: As my Alzheimer's authority told me, caregivers count. Protect yourself. Have a plan.

Venting: Think about how you deal with a friend or relative who vents to you. You may just listen and say, "There, there," or maybe you offer what you think is valuable advice. Regardless of how close you are, you will eventually tire of a person who is constantly calling to share his or her unhappiness. That's when venting becomes whining. So you yourself, as a person under great stress may need to share the daily challenges of your situation with a professional. Venting to a professional is a much better idea. A counselor is, first, one whose purpose is to listen; second, a counselor who deals with dementia/Alzheimer's will have valuable suggestions.

Weird Stuff: You may notice strange goings- on around the house. If your LO unloads the dishwasher, he or she may put stuff away in places you never dreamed these items could be put!

If your LO loads the dishwasher, the load may include things that shouldn't go in (crystal, sharp knives, etc.)

If your LO hand-washes stuff, he/she will eventually forget to use soap, resulting in greasy bowls, platters, etc. It just requires checking the cleanliness of all items before you use them again.

My LO hoards white washcloths in his sock drawer. I have no idea why. When too many wash cloths disappear into the drawer, I just remove a few and put them back in the linen closet.

Work: Do you work outside the home? That can be a blessing or a stressor. It gives you a reason, out side of your caregiving role, to get up and get going in the morning. If you are working, you are probably with other adults who do not have dementia. You are bringing home a paycheck, which you may badly need.

You also may feel guilty about being away from your LO and fear that something may happen to him or her while you are not there.

How long can you reasonably be gone from the house? Does your LO have to be medicated at a certain time?

Talk to your employer. Is there a possibility you can split your work day between your work office and your home office?

Would it make sense to take an early retirement or go to a part-time position?

After you have had the conversation with your boss, it's time to have the conversation with the family. Even if you continue to work, you may need a little financial help, and they may be able to provide it. Ask.

X'es on the calendar: This can help your LO keep up with the days that are gone and the ones to come.

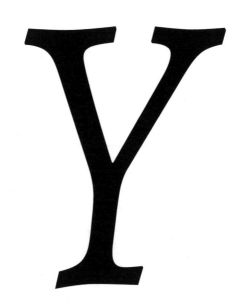

Yours, Mine & Ours: After you have organized and clarified your financial house, it's time to look at the stuff in your home. Have you considered what your living arrangements will be as your LO's dementia progresses? Will you stay in your home together? Will you "downsize" together? Will you stay in your home if your LO needs to be moved to an assisted living/memory care facility? And, what if something happens to you (illness, injury or death) at a time when your LO is dependent upon you?

Consider this approach:

Look at all the possessions in your attic, garage basement and closets.

Ask yourself why all this stuff is stored away in your attic, garage, basement or closet and isn't being used?

Ask yourself whether you'd want to pack, move and unpack this stuff if you had to move.

Ask yourself who would like to have your stuff.

BULLETIN!!!!!

No one wants your stuff. I can say this with confidence! No one, whether related to you or not, wants your stuff. Really. And no one wants your mother's stuff either.

I hate to be the one to break it to you, but the coming generations don't live like Baby Boomers live.

They don't want old stuff. Period. Move on.

Get rid of everything you don't use.

I got a lot of pushback from my LO when I suggested we clean up the work bench area, which in our house is a closet with louvered doors. When you open doors and things fall out on your head, it's time to clean them out. But, no, all that stuff was valuable, my LO insisted. Every tool, screw or landline cable had special meaning to my LO. But, no one, and I mean NO ONE needs 24 hammers.

So, with the idea of having to move this stuff weighing on my mind, I began a secretive editing of stuff, one small trash bag at a time. Understand, my LO never used these items, nor did he visit he workbench area with any regularity, so "editing" wasn't too difficult as long as he didn't see me do it.

When I finally showed him a very tidy workbench area, he was delighted. He hasn't opened those doors since.

If there are things you want to give to relatives or friends at some future date, indicate your wishes in your will and be sure to secure them in a special place.

If it's little mementos you want a certain person to have, get a plastic container, with a lid, for each recipient. Put their name on the top and each time you decide to give them something, put it in the tub. Some tubs will be larger than other tubs.

Then, when you do move to smaller quarters or heaven, THEY can figure out what to do with their stuff!

Organizing, editing and disposing of stuff can be a project to enjoy with your LO unless he is unreasonably attached to his hammers. In that case, I recommend you start eliminating stuff one small trash bag at a time!

ZEST: It took me a while to come up with this one. If having a zest for life does not come naturally to you, this is the time to try it.! When your LO exclaims in frustration about being stupid or useless, it's up to you to turn it around. Tell them him or her how lucky you both are to have each other, or what a beautiful day it is. Make day- to- day chores an activity you can do together. My Mother and I could have fun in a traffic jam. I swear she could entertain herself and others around her with a rubber band.

When a recipe calls for the zest of a lemon, lime or orange, the resulting food just tastes better, fuller. You are the one who will have to add the zest to the recipe of your life. For you and your LO.

Resources

The best resource I have found is www.alz.org. There you can navigate their virtual library, support services, and other really good information.

Also, check out your state's board or department for aging.

Seniornavigator.org is a Virginia-based website with lots of helpful information, where ever the caregiver may reside.

Acknowledgements

In the course of one week, four people told me I should write a book about my life with a dementia patient. So, I did. Thanks to the four of you: Sue Freidman, Rita Mae Brown, Susan Terwilleger and Jane Rund.

Thanks also to my dear friends, Mary T. Miller, Jane Goodman and Meredith Strohm-Gunter.

Many thanks to my sisters, Marjorie, Elizabeth and Amy for your support and encouragement. And daily phone calls, texts and emails.

Marijean Oldham patiently guided me into Blog World.

And many thanks to my sister-in-law, Adele Foy. Her thoughtful and skillful editing resulted in something readable!